AMAZING ANIMALS

BIGHORN SHEEP

BY KATE RIGGS

CREATIVE EDUCATION • CREATIVE PAPERBACKS

Published by Creative Education
and Creative Paperbacks
P.O. Box 227, Mankato, Minnesota 56002
Creative Education and Creative Paperbacks
are imprints of The Creative Company
www.thecreativecompany.us

Design by The Design Lab
Production by Rachel Klimpel
Art direction by Rita Marshall
Printed in the United States of America

Photographs by 123RF (pinkcandy), Alamy (All Canada
Photos, Allen Thornton, John E Marriott, robertharding,
William Mullins), Corbis (Jeff Vanuga, Sumio Harada/Min-
den Pictures), Depositphotos (jill@ghostbear.org), Dream-
stime (Anankkml), Getty (CR Courson), iStock (KenRinger,
Petr Kahanek, raincoast), Shutterstock (Sarah Jessup,
Wesley Aston)

Library of Congress Cataloging-in-Publication Data
Names: Riggs, Kate, author. Title: Bighorn sheep / by Kate
Riggs. Description: Mankato, Minnesota: The Creative
Company, [2023] | Series: Amazing animals | Includes
bibliographical references and index. | Audience: Ages
6–9 | Audience: Grades 2–3 | Summary: "Elementary-
aged readers will discover how bighorn sheep stay safe
from predators. Full color images and clear explanations
highlight the habitat, diet, and lifestyle of these fascinat-
ing mountain creatures."– Provided by publisher. Identi-
fiers: LCCN 2021053395 (print) | LCCN 2021053396
(ebook) | ISBN 9781640265608 (hardcover) | ISBN
9781682771150 (paperback) | ISBN 9781640006799
(adobe pdf)
Subjects: LCSH: Bighorn sheep–Juvenile literature.
Classification: LCC QL737.U53 R5456 2023 (print)
| LCC QL737.U53 (ebook) | DDC 599.649–dc23/
eng/20211203
LC record available at https://lccn.loc.gov/2021053395
LC ebook record available at https://lccn.loc.
gov/2021053396

Table of Contents

There are five kinds of desert bighorn sheep.

Bighorn sheep are some of the largest wild sheep in the world. There are at least three **subspecies**. They all live in North America.

subspecies a group of similar (or closely related) animals within a larger group, called a species

Bighorns are known for their curled horns. Males and females have horns. The horns are hard and made of bone. They do not fall off like deer antlers do. Mountain bighorn sheep have the largest horns. The horns weigh almost 30 pounds (13.6 kg)!

Male bighorns have curlier horns than females.

Mountain bighorns

are larger than desert bighorns. A male mountain bighorn can weigh 300 pounds (136 kg). Females usually weigh around 200 pounds (91 kg). All bighorns eat more in summer. They lose weight in winter. There is not as much food then.

A bighorn's furry coat keeps it warm in the mountains.

Mountain bighorn sheep live in the Rockies and Sierra Nevada. Desert bighorns are found in hot, dry places. Many live in states like California and Utah.

From young to old, bighorns climb their rocky homes.

Bighorn sheep eat dry grass and sticks. During summer they also eat flowers. They spend a lot of time eating. The way they feed is called grazing.

Sheep have special stomachs that help them eat tough plants.

About 5 to 15 females, lambs, and young bighorns live in a herd.

One lamb is born to a female bighorn in late spring. It has dark eyes and tiny horns. When it is about three weeks old, it joins other lambs. They play and rest together in a group called a nursery herd. All the mothers and their young live in a bigger herd.

lamb a baby bighorn sheep

Bighorn sheep can run quickly. They can go 30 miles (48.3 km) per hour on flat land. They can walk on rocks and jump far.

On a rocky mountain, bighorns can run 15 miles (24.1 km) per hour.

Bighorns need a ledge only two inches (5.1 cm) wide to stay safe.

Bighorns run away from predators. They climb rocky ledges to reach safe spots. Mountain lions, wolves, and other animals cannot reach bighorn sheep there.

predators animals that kill and eat other animals

People who live near bighorns may see these sheep a lot. You can visit national parks to see bighorns and other animals in the wild. Keep your distance! Bighorns may charge if you get too close.

A bighorn in summer will shed its thick winter fur.

A Bighorn Sheep Tale

There is a story about how the bighorn sheep got its curly horns. A long time ago, Bighorn had straight horns. He was using them to push animals over a cliff! Coyote pushed Bighorn back but saved him by grabbing his horns. When Coyote let go, the horns curled up. They have been curled ever since.

Read More

Hudak, Heather C. *Let's Explore Mountains*. Mankato: The Child's World, 2022.

Messner, Kate. *Over and Under the Canyon*. San Francisco: Chronicle Books, 2021.

Websites

DK FindOut! Bighorn Sheep Facts
https://www.dkfindout.com/us/animals-and-nature/cattle/bighorn-sheep/
This interactive site has more bighorn sheep facts.

National Park Service: Bighorn Sheep
https://www.nps.gov/yell/learn/nature/bighorn-sheep.htm
Learn more about the bighorn sheep in Yellowstone National Park.

Note: Every effort has been made to ensure that the websites listed above are suitable for children, that they have educational value, and that they contain no inappropriate material. However, because of the nature of the Internet, it is impossible to guarantee that these sites will remain active indefinitely or that their contents will not be altered.

Index